About the Author

A medical doctor by profession. A traveller and a writer by passion. Working as medical director of a firm in Kuwait.

My Letters to the Butterfly

Dr Haneesh Khani

My Letters to the Butterfly

Vanguard Press

VANGUARD PAPERBACK

© Copyright 2023
Dr Haneesh Khani

The right of Dr Haneesh Khani to be identified as author of this
work has been asserted by thim in accordance with the
Copyright, Designs and Patents Act 1988.

All Rights Reserved

No reproduction, copy or transmission of this publication
may be made without written permission.
No paragraph of this publication may be reproduced,
copied or transmitted save with the written permission of the
publisher, or in accordance with the provisions
of the Copyright Act 1956 (as amended).

Any person who commits any unauthorised act in relation to
this publication may be liable to criminal
prosecution and civil claims for damages.

A CIP catalogue record for this title is
available from the British Library.

ISBN 978 1 80016 891 6

*Vanguard Press is an imprint of
Pegasus Elliot Mackenzie Publishers Ltd.*
www.pegasuspublishers.com

First Published in 2023

**Vanguard Press
Sheraton House Castle Park
Cambridge England**

Printed & Bound in Great Britain

To all my fellow human beings.

Author's Note

Dear friend,

   I hope you are fine and well. A butterfly is a beautiful being.

   From an egg to caterpillar, from caterpillar to chrysalis, from chrysalis to an adult; the butterfly undergoes a lot of struggles to emerge as a beautiful flying being. Life is like that. Nobody said that life would be easy. GOD has created every living being in a miraculous way, so that every living being is different and very special. Every human life is different from another. Everyone is tested differently and individually by the trials and signs, so that we emerge as strong as a butterfly, an eagle or a phoenix; depending on our focus, effort, willpower and hard work. A butterfly never thinks about the thorns when it focuses on the flower. Humans have an attitude of worrying about the thorns instead of smiling at the flower. A human has a mixture of emotions and they are only complete with their strengths along with their weaknesses. We have been created by GOD in a very special form so that all the other living beings are created to support or entertain us, and they are special in their own ways. Apart from humans, all other living beings follow signs to move forward silently and happily. Human beings question a lot, even when the universe has signs of the answers around them. It's a matter of the viewpoints toward life.

Once, a butterfly reached out to me when I was travelling in God's own country, KERALA. She was so beautiful. We met while we both were following signs. She was searching for her own soul. When I learned of her search, I told her that we both have the same soul and it's a part of our CREATOR's soul.

"So, was I searching for GOD?" she asked me. I nodded, "YES." She flew to another flower. The flower whispered to her that they both have the same soul. Wherever she flew and whomever she met, she learned that all souls belong to ONE and they all are ONE.

That was the greatest answer to her, and at that point, I decided to name this book as *'MY LETTERS TO THE BUTTERFLY,'* because we, the living beings, all have the same soul from the greatest soul, our ALMIGHTY.

This book is the result of my experiences, thoughts, signs, trials and silences; through which I intent to give a helping hand to all fellow humans whom this book reaches, according to the great script of the ALMIGHTY. If it touches your beautiful heart, if it gives strength to you, if it helps you win your goals and dreams; I'm grateful. Never give up on life. Be strong alone. Be your best friend. Believe in miracles, and be a miracle. Be a beautiful butterfly and spread your love, beauty, and kindness so that when you are with the right flower, let your synergy attract more beauty to the universe that lies deep within and around you.

Let's not separate based on religion, caste, colour, creed, possessions, profession, gender or any manner. Let's unite. Let's be one so that THE ONE who sent us according to his purpose will be the happiest. This is a moment of thanksgiving to the great ONE and the whole of his creation, whom I have met in this short and beautiful journey of my blessed life. Without you, I would not have learned so well. Without the experiences given by you, I would not have been so much strong. Here I'm dedicating my first book, which with a few words conveys the deeper meanings of the realities of life to each and every one of you. I'm not trying to teach you anything here. I'm just trying to awaken you.

Thanking you all once again.
With Love,
Dr HANEESH KHANI

Introduction

This is the thing about the human spirit. No matter how far you have dipped yourself in pain, no matter how far darkness has pulled you close, the human spirit always finds a light to keep strong, to gather themselves, to take them home. This book is truly your beacon of light, it is a gentle reminder, it will reel you home whenever you find yourself lost. Allow it to pave a path to your true self. Allow it to guide you to live a joy-filled life.

I have been so profoundly touched by the intentions set by Dr Haneesh Khani and the message this book carries. You are about to embark on this very special journey, offered to you by the most spiritual and authentic person. Dr Han (we travellers call him by that name) is truly a gift. His kindness through his philanthropic work and his willingness to make positive changes never fails to instil hope. And this book offers you exactly that; a glimpse of hope. I am so thrilled that you are holding this book in your hands at this moment. In this world so relentless, the message of the book is simply to slow down and appreciate every fibre of your being. In doing so, it allows you to be guided by your heart, to release stress from everyday life and to trust your intuition, to lead a fulfilled life, crafted by you. You truly are a miracle. Place this book on your nightstand. Let it be your guide, a haven, a talisman.

Thursday, 24 March 2022. This is one of the miracles that took place in my life, and I am so grateful. Thank you, Dr Han, for allowing me to say a few words in this very special book. I find myself very fortunate.

Mika Myrie

Cambridge, England.

To practice your dreams, you must love yourself. You must live for yourself. In solitude is where real talent grows up, in silence. This sort of person doesn't rush.

They trust the process. They never give up. The world calls them winners.

Anything that is repeated goes deeper into the consciousness.

That's why prayers, holy verses, and advice are repeated again and again. This book also repeats many things at the apt moments. The motive is to help you to get deeper into the real meanings and the reality of the consciousness.

Look around. You may see the sad ones, the lonely. Look at those broken ones with love. Hold the hands of the weary, look up and smile. You will feel a joy within you. That's called the real happiness.

The hardest test is having the patience to wait for the right moment. But it's worth it. Follow the signs happily.

A smile is the result, from the Creator.

Who you are becoming is more important than who you have been. All things are sometimes difficult before they become easy. Do not give up.

    Keep going.

Wake up with a purpose. Live the days with compassion. Feel the result of your deeds in the night. Thank the Almighty with love. Count every breath as a blessing. Sleep with a beautiful smile. Rise up again with a purpose.

What you observe, what you see, what you follow, what you think, what you feel, what you relate, what you grab, is what you become.

Choose wisely.

Struggles are one of the perfect kinds of blessings. They make you strong. They deepen your faith. Remember, with every difficulty there is a relief. However, grow in silence. Let your silences shape you to be a beautiful being.

Neither judge, nor pass judgement. The person whom you are assessing could also be the one who will shape you into a beautiful ray of the light. Your judgement may occasionally prevent you from finding 'pathways' of peace, happiness and many more realities.

    Learn from life well
    &
    live it wisely.

The letter 'K' is important in the English alphabet due to the word KINDNESS. That word cannot be fully described. It is lived. It is felt. It is understood just like another word: LOVE. He who is kind is more lovely.

To write, you might have thought a lot. To think, you might have experienced a lot. To experience, you might have travelled a lot. To travel, you might have read a lot. To read, you might have learned a lot. To learn, you might have said YES to a lot.

SAY YES TO LIFE!

Willingness is the key to success.

Game-changers in life.

1) Faith
2) Gratitude
3) Forgiveness
4) Kindness
5) Believing in yourself
6) Confidence
7) Willpower
8) Understanding
9) Trials
10) Patience
11) Attitude
12) Humility
13) Love
14) Self respect
15) Discipline

Live more of a different kind of life. A new thought-pattern.

A new way. Another try. A good old dream modified to reality; or it can be anything whatsoever

RAISE your standards, so that everything in your life will RISE to meet you.

The forty rules of love explained by RUMI and SHAMZ TABREZI gathered to acknowledge that each of them started their 'journey' to describe one mighty word. That word was LOVE. Be wise. Be in LOVE with YOURSELF too.

Every trial you face gives a new lesson to learn from. Some blame it. Some smile because of it, and some wonder at it. There are different ones who follow the signs and try to wonder differently. They create based on experiences, lessons and situations. A 'winner' is what you decide to be.

FIND A WAY. DON'T FADE AWAY.

Do yourself a huge favour: never compare yourself to anyone. Be your own best version. 'The happiest one.'

The lovely one. Let your endorphins smile. When you realise what life means, you are just watching the show. You never rush the process. A winner is also a loser who tried once more.

Work on things which people are unable to take away from you. Your dreams, knowledge, patience, happiness, lifestyle, meditation, prayer, attitude, mindset, personality, and your entire being. Success is when preparation meets opportunities.
PREPARE DIFFERENTLY.

A change is always necessary at the right moment in life. When you change, your surroundings turn beautiful. Patience adds a lot of colours to those chances of being different. If necessary, change the direction. There might be a new view toward your destined path. Walk it gratefully.

Use your energy to heal, believe, trust and grow. The time wasted by judging others might be the real time for the 'growth' of the self. Don't just settle for who you are and what you are. EVOLVE. You can rise by yourself or by lifting the saddened.

    I tried both.

Never prove anything to anyone. Prove it to your heart and soul. Remember, not everyone will have the same standard and thoughts. So, as much you are trying to prove yourself to anyone, you are wasting the chance to do something better. The wise will understand even the silences.

Make people think.

Never allow someone to define you except GOD. Learn to live beautiful stories in everyday life. Try to find a different you, which happens when you become a better version of yourself day by day. Don't argue. Question yourself, so that your findings will let you create a new way to a bright future. Be silent and listen.

The duration between your wisdom and an upcoming opportunity is a beautiful process. Until then, exercise, meditate, pray, help, heal, accept, give, forgive, dream, dance, read, write, learn, listen, travel, rest, relax, smile and live happily.

Kindly value your peace. Rise up with more potential. You are amazing.

The wind is sent ahead of miracles. It strengthens your heart to follow signs. The skies add rains, stars dance and clouds shape things. Lightening or thunder might accompany the process. That's called life. While it storms, faith and confidence will help you fly.

    Enjoy the flight of life.

Be like a rock in a storm. Be a butterfly while the winds blow. Be the one who swims against the current, the humble one who lift others up and be the smile of the ones around you. Be a soul who understands, the ear that listens, the hands which give and the heart that forgives. Be the one with a different spark.

FIND THAT BEAUTIFUL YOU.

Do you know why GOD created the heart to sit to the left side? It is for you to think right. The 'right' to be imperfect. The right to be the happy you. The right to never give up. When you say yes to life, you may realise that RIGHT has many meanings.

The possibilities circling you are infinite. Your purpose is to relax and find a way to reach them. Patience is a necessity. Hope is a friend.

Confidence is the booster dose. Trials are the stepping stones. Signs become ropes to climb. Kindness keeps the heart alive. Faith creates miracles and you become a warrior.

The promise of love hides in a territory called understanding. There is not much value for love, without understanding the one whom you love. Love is a feeling. Love is kind. Love is freedom.

Love is the real energy.

Love is the way to ALMIGHTY. Be on that way back to him.

When the universe gives you a new beginning, write a new story. A different kind. A promising one. Let it be so beautiful that one night when you look back, you might realise that the new you achieved a lot more than your dreams. Miracles will find a way back to your heart to whisper...

Yes, you can do more!

When the heart is soft and thoughts are open, acceptance of new lessons result in a fine bonding with the universe. Once it is bound, you need to nurture it with confidence and gratitude. As you start to walk in that way, the rhythm of life brings happiness, miracles, optimism, peace and prosperity. Have a wise journey.

Life is a collective experience which can adapt to many circumstances, beautiful signs and trials. Trials become the path towards your next level. When you reach that level, look down on the path which helped you to climb high. You might see another one struggling there. Help that one.

It is called love.

If you really want something in life, go and achieve it. People may judge. Never mind. The ONE who created all the past and current legends himself has also created you; who tests you with all the connected vibrations of the entire living and non-living beings of the universe and beyond. Win the tests silently. Rise up proud and wise.

Dream big. Struggle hard. Play well. Understand silently. Wait patiently. Act accordingly. Smile soulfully. "Remember that human is imperfect". Modify your imperfections into creativity so that it becomes a perfect creativity. When you change into a new you, even the mistakes become experiences.

Many of the disputes you experience will disappear when you stop telling people what's going on in your life. Your happiness spreads deep into your soul and body when you realise the purpose of your life. When that purpose is accepted by your heart, it starts a new type of pulse. A pulse of a humble smile of satisfaction.

Whenever you feel you are struggling or stranded, remember that a new way is opening. The struggle you experience could be a stepping stone for a new zone. Never change the infrastructure. Instead, modify that zone into a lovely one of soulful creativities.

Be wise. Be the help.

Be the difference. You will live miracles.

Your body is the only place where you live. The rest is just part and parcel of a beautiful journey to find out your life's purpose. Walk the life as if you are a student of eternity. Never let anybody know completely the wisdom you attain silently. Keep the secret of the signs safe within you. Others may not understand.

It's not their cup of tea.

He is wiser.
Who?
GOD. Who else?

When you start speaking to yourself, you start loving the process of the miracles of life. Silence speaks in four ways. You become clever when you speak to your brain. When it is to the heart, you turn kind. To the mind, it is experience, and when it is done to your soul, you are speaking to GOD.

Be wise. Feel blessed.
Your soul is from GOD'S soul.

The thought process in life starts from the questions you raise during your childhood. Until a moment in life, you keep questioning others. Wisdom arises when you question yourself silently. Then, a stage arrives when you get the answers as SIGNS from the universe even without questions. That becomes the zone of guidance from GOD.

Go forward.

You will find more of you.

Being open and respectful are essential parts of synergy.

The sweetness of a relationship hides in the humility of the individual. The individual becomes a real team leader if, and only if, he supports the team by projecting each one of his teammates towards a new level of creativity. Then, it is called humanism. Humanism has a lot of meanings.

Having a beautiful meaning is an essential part of life that arises when you are ready to love silences. Patience doesn't exist where there is no silence. Silence still exists in a beautiful conversation if you are a good listener. The listener always becomes the winner of many hearts.

So, learn, practice, love and live meanings.

Meanings make a human lovable.

The wise understand that everything happens for a reason. Remember, if you are alive and peaceful you can do more. An incident is a test for many people in different ways. Be wise and stay away from arguments. Being happy is the most amazing kindness you can gift to yourself. You are special, gifted and blessed.
Keep smiling.

Successful people are not just gifted or lucky. They work hard, find their purpose, wait for the signs and then succeed with their purpose. Anything and everything has a reason in life. When you find that reason, you are close to life's meaning. When you grab that meaning, you realised a purpose. That path will lead you to more purposes for a meaningful life and victories.

Don't compete with anyone. Don't be jealous of anyone. Don't argue with anyone. Because one day, you might look back and realise that you worried a lot about things that really don't matter. Remove yourself from anywhere you don't feel valued and just focus on becoming the best version of yourself.

You are valuable.

You are beautiful.

Rest, recovery, reflection and peace are essential parts of a happy and successful life. You may not get what you like and that's fine. Sweat out today for a wonderful present to create a beautiful tomorrow.

Don't get carried away by the limelight. Keep your feet and heart always grounded. You will be a twinkling star in the hearts of the right people.

One year of hardcore alignment and focus can put you six years ahead in life. There is a power in consistency and determination.

Be wise enough to listen to what a person is NOT saying. Suffer the pain of the discipline. Never suffer by doubting yourself. Harness your power, skill and knowledge. Exceed your limits and the expectation of others. You are unstoppable. Keep going.

A positive mind finds opportunity in everything. But sometimes you must understand the negatives too. That describes a part of the process of learning life.

You have to struggle to learn about life. You must experience the pros and cons. Keep your struggles secret until you succeed and then keep it even more private. Sometimes success and happiness are secret.

Learn to embrace the storms in your life. A road of yours cannot be walked by others, especially in your shoes. Believe in yourself. Believe in sudden positive shifts. Believe that everything is in your favour and try hard.

Things can change for you any time. Learn to relax in between. Learn to smile at any trials. Your smile is more beautiful when you feel it with your heart.

Gratitude can be shown even for breathing fresh air. Happiness cannot exist without gratitude. It helps you to feel humble. It helps you understand that GOD's help is always there for you, and you are never alone. Whatever you do, he adds his part to it. It cannot be explained. It's a feeling and a beautiful reality which must be understood by the receiver of the blessings. It is like you remember your LORD for whatever comes your way, and you are assured that he will put you in safe zone with love and care.

Secrets are a part of the journey of life. Since childhood you start the habit of revealing your secrets to the ones around you. Teenage years showed you different results of revealing secrets. Adulthood helped you realise that secrets are a way to realise best friends.

Later, there comes a stage called maturity, where you will reveal your secrets to no one, and you get success in life. When you succeed, hide more of the 'secrets to victory.'

Love is the emotion which binds the whole universe. Love is the best form of energy, which can be transferred to heal others. Love is the starting point of life from the creator to the mother's womb, then it becomes the sign of happiness, and later the trial to understand and learn the mastery of life. Then at a beautiful turning point, love becomes non-materialistic when it turns towards the ALMIGHTY. Love is the most sacred emotion, especially the love of ALMIGHTY and the love towards ALMIGHTY.

Never try to coerce or control anything or anyone. The universe has a way of connecting processes so that something must happen in its own way, which you may never expect. Challenge yourself to control the way in which you respond to the incidents around you instead of controlling others. You don't need power to love. To love someone, you just need love.

You didn't bring anything to this world. You got everything free since birth. You were loved, cared for, helped and nourished by parents, relatives and society. At a turning point during the adulthood, you start to live the same theme of helping others. When you start that journey, try a different theme to help you and to help others around you. Nourish it with love, water it with kindness, spread the fragrance of care and create a lovely different journey. You will see a lot of paradises at the end of that journey.

There is no fear in success. Fear is just an emotion which holds you back from a beautiful and happy life. Without risks, life is not a challenging reality.

A journey without challenges is just a normal one, like many others. Be courageous enough to fight the war of silence and wisdom.

Be Different, Be Victorious.

From the depths of the darkness, the first light will be your insight to never give up. When you decide to move forward you will receive a beautiful ray of light from the signs of the universe.

That creates a smile when the rays align with the beautiful rays of your insight. The journey may be hard at first. Don't worry. Pull yourself together and move forward. Heavens are waiting for you on that journey.

Keep going.

Try to understand people before trusting them. You don't always have to agree with one another. What is more important is that you learn to respect each other. Believe in debates more than arguments. Debate has synergy while argument is destructive. Never expect to get what you give, even if it is a nice word. The real education reflects in your behaviour and attitude.

It defines you.

Be well defined.

Your greatest mistake is to search for your happiness in others. That will sadden you. Search for it in yourself so that you will be the strongest even when you are left alone.

Loneliness and solitude have entirely different meanings. Lonely is what others make you feel but solitude is your preference to grow more.

The wise will embrace solitude. Choose your friends wisely and make it a very small circle. When you have amazing friends, even the failures look beautiful.

Try to be your own best companion.

That adds more to your journey.

Be thankful for all the people who said no to you. Because of them you searched the reasons to find out many YESES in your life to reach your position and wisdom from eternity. Believe in miracles and prepare well to admire them. You will live miracles when your insight is better than your eyesight. When the insight is a proven one, you get every answer from the universe to make sure that your future is bright and fine. Struggle and practice now to smile anytime. Be a Warrior!!

Trust your intuition. Most of the time it will be true.

Stop overthinking. Don't try to control everything. Just let it be and you will be happy. Never be afraid. A head full of fear has no space for love, wisdom and dreams. Fear not the intuition, instead gain answers from it. Use everything as learning material to practice life. When you are afraid, you are dead while being alive. Don't take orders from people, instead aim to be independent.

If you are comfortable alone, you are a powerful individual.

That strength reached you through the wonderful experiences in life. It helps you to get moulded into a beautiful creature who knows how to rise whenever you fall. That's the most important lesson in anyone's life. Even when you get hurt, spread positivity and patience. If you could spread love as quickly as they spread hate and negativity, this world would have been so amazing.

Life is too short to waste time with those who doesn't respect you. Surround yourself with people who inspire you to smile, are inspired by you. Heal, help and care for the genuine ones. Help yourself to be an eagle of your own kind. Once you are strong, you can help more. The best way towards a better life is by healing yourself.

Don't take advantage of others. Never start a relationship for material gains. Don't lie to yourself.

Follow your heart and you will learn how to follow signs.

Follow signs and you will realise that you were following your heart. Both are connected in a beautiful way. Signs are the pulse of the universe. If you can align your heartbeats with it, the result will be an impulse of happiness. Try it, receive it and smile at life.

"So, lose not heart, nor fall into despair, for you will be superior if you are true in faith."

To every call, GOD answers many times, "Hi I'm here." When you truly believe in what you are doing, it shows, and pay well in many ways. Winners are always excited in peace about where they are going. Stay strong and make them wonder how you are still smiling. Words are silent in front of powerful smile. Your smile is your answer.

Each day is a new start. Each moment is a new opportunity. Each breath is a new blessing. Treat each one who comes to you as a special guest. The good or the bad, everyone serves a purpose to reshape you. Everything happens for a reason. Speak humble, listen wisely, help kindly and attach carefully. Trust actions more than words. When you are nice to people, GOD's mercy never reach an end.

Life tests a person in many ways. Sometimes it tests by nothing and some other times it tests by everything happening to a person at once. Whatever the situation, never give up. When you are comfortable, growth is static. Get out of the comfort zone so that you can grow. Your growth can help many poor people around you. So, never lose the chance to grow and do better to the people. You can also grow by helping others.

Not everyone is going to understand your journey. It's fine and it is a blessing that you don't need to explain it. Take things positively and live your everyday signs and goals well. Make a wish list according to your wishes and signs so that you can try to find out what will come your way. When you follow signs well, you will realise that everything is beautifully falling into place. That will be start of a real journey.

You can completely recreate yourself and rise from anything. Have some new thoughts. Learn something new. Adapt new habits. Travel to new destinations. Accept silences. Choose wisely and realise that you are not stuck. Be your own light to see through the darkness, then the universe will add light to your path. Remember, all the darkness cannot hide even a single ray of light.

Keep going.

The past is a closed chapter which cannot be opened or rewritten in any way. That time is over. Never look back with a lot of regret. Remember the lessons and apply it on the path of the present to create a beautiful way to your future. Most of the time, you are your guide. Your soul knows when something is authentic, true, wise and real. No matter who tries to persuade you off, trust your feelings. Choose love as your strength during your journey and no one can stop you.

Be happy because you can see the good side of everything. Be silent because you can get answers without questions. When the time is right, something great will cross your path unexpectedly. Don't rush things. Whatever has to happen will happen in its own time. You have been through a lot and it's time for you to shine. Better days are on the way. Get ready.

There are many colourful flowers on the path of life, but the prettiest have the sharpest thorns. A butterfly never looks at the thorns. It focuses on the flower and adds beauty to it. So much of your happiness depends on how you choose to look at the world. Peace is not the absence of troubles, but the presence of wisdom. Be doers of the word and not hearers only.

Life is what you make it.

Hold fast to hope. Trust GOD. Everything is going to be fine. Always be thankful to GOD, as he serves all your needs. When the love of GOD is there with you, no one can stop you from being blessed. Start every journey with happiness and faith. The first step toward getting somewhere is to realise that you are not going to stay where you are now. Be wise. Be happy.

Be courageous. Be a backpacker.

A mind which is sick with anger will not benefit from wisdom. Wisdom arises when you learn how to control your reactions to incidents that trigger your soul. Humans were created by GOD to undergo tests and to become strong. So, trust that process. Never surrender in hardships. Have faith and rise from every fall. The best feeling in the world is watching things finally fall into place after watching them falling apart for so long.

When fortune gives you a chance to prove yourself, you barely have a handful of days to prepare. In exchange it asks for every drop of your preparations and sweat. So, prepare and sweat well in between the process of the journey to the opportunity so that, when opportunity arrives at your doors, you can win with ease. In between, your behaviour is the determining factor towards the victory. Fortune bows in front of your intense effort.

A person who is happy with what the ALMIGHTY provides for him will enjoy peace of mind, satisfaction and tranquillity. Make a friendship from the skies about which even the earth feels happy. That's the friendship of the ALMIGHTY. If you are content with what he has given to you, you are the richest person. The rest what is coming to you isa bonus in this life. This world has many lies. Truth is your bond with the CREATOR.

When the heart is filled with storms of questions, put them together into a pond called patience so that your wisdom will show answers in the form of signs from the universe. Hold strong to your dreams. Don't pay heed to what others say. Your day is arriving. Prove your point to yourself and not to others.

Explanations kills the reality of signs and dreams.

When you expect anything from others, you experience a negative energy during the entire process of that expectation period.

It occurs due to a materialistic possessive attitude. Once a friend told me a beautiful reality. Expect nothing and accept everything. That's your miracle. I agreed to it in that moment.

Heaven is here on this beautiful planet too. It depends on how you accept and react to the circumstances around you. When you try to see the good in everything, the heaven is near to you. Once you realise that, you get adapted slowly into the process of connections and vibrations of the universe. Trust that process peacefully so that you can design more than heavens. Thank the ALMIGHTY and create heavens.

Everyone is walking their own journey and dreams. Try to be a small part of others' dreams and happiness, so that you can watch your own dreams reaching you as a miracle. When you help, you will feel a river flowing in you, a joy. Your happiness is designed and defined by the one within you.

Help and be happy,

Stop comparing yourself with people who started years before you. Focus on your own journey. You have your own race to win, and your journey is different from the entire creation's. Practice like you have won already. Perform like you have never lost. Finish the game well and smile at the image in your mirror. When the time is right, whatever you do or feel will turn out alright.

All the pain that you endured have a purpose. Without a doubt, every difficulty in your life, whether it is big or small, is something that will produce faith, strength, peace and perseverance in you. Accept that reality. Be stronger and more peaceful. Be your best buddy. Be more wonderful.

In life, what we really want will never come easy. GOD always make a better way to reach our goals. It's a beautiful process. Trust him. Never give up. A lot more is to come on your path before your last breath. Good things happen at the right moment and the right moment is when you receive the real answers. A phoenix never surrenders to failures.

From your merciful CREATOR, you get more than what you wish for. Be grateful for every minute thing. Thank everyone in your life for the talks, the walks, the hugs, the smiles, the fights, the thorns, the pros and the cons. Thank each moment for the beautiful and amazing visuals of life. Everything helped you to be the new you of today and now. Look back gratefully and smile at the past.

You will find different types of lives in everyone. Different characters. Different dreams.

Different moods. Different qualities. Different types of trusts, beliefs and smiles. When all the creation is different, never let anyone tell you to be like someone else. Your beauty is to be different. Winners do things differently.

Sometimes the people with the greatest potential often take the longest to find their path because, their creativity is a double-edged sword. It lives and hides at the heart of their brilliance. When they prove themselves, the world realises that they are different. Fall in love with your own brilliance. Fall in love with caring yourself. Fall in love with becoming the finest version of yourself, but with passion, compassion, patience and respect toward your own journey.

Experiences teach you the real meaning of a beautiful and calm life. Never look back and get stuck in sadness. You are unable to change the past. Leave it and move on with new goals. Be engaged in something important and leave all the unnecessary things aside. The good thing is that we aren't being penalized for handling our purpose late. Do well.

Whatever happens, never worry much in life. Stop for a while, pause for a while more, get a few fresh deep breaths, thank the ALMIGHTY and start again with more enthusiasm from the scratches. Never care about what others think. Never try to impress others. Just care about how you feel. There will be a turning point at a definite moment.

Learn more about anything that seems important to you. Never waste time in unnecessary things. Distance yourself from everything giving you a negative energy. Never let anyone know about your real dreams. Never strive for anything which is not yours. Life has worth in each moment. After all, life is the best teacher. Learn it well.

Everything that happened in your life was written by the CREATOR to help you find the real purpose of your life to redefine a new you. Learn more and, moreover, exercise your brain and heart by being consistent in lessons and by forgiveness. Never shed your energy thinking about your past. Life is now, and it is a gift to you. The future is a beautiful dream, and when you never give up, the dreams turn into a beautiful reality.

Sometimes you may feel that you are being pulled in different directions. That happens to place you at the right path hidden among all the other directions, so that you can experience the reality of guidance. Be in the company of mature people; those who admit that they are wrong. Those who don't blame others for their mistakes. Those who take responsibility for their actions. Those people will help you grow. They won't let you down. They will smile at your triumphs. Choose your friends wisely.

Don't end up like a loser by being a procrastinator. Don't put off to the next day what you should do today. When you have the habit of procrastinating you will miss many opportunities that the ALMIGHTY has sent to you through the universe on your path of the journey. Don't refuse to see what is dangling in front of you right now. Don't refuse the blessings by procrastination.

Never put people down. Pray for them instead.

Motivate, empower and encourage people so that, they can rise at the right moments. If you find someone solo and strong, realise that they are very special. Solitude is the place where real purpose comes into life. Do the right thing for you and the people around you. When the time is right, miracles will pave the way for you.

You can change the world around you by your example, not by your opinion. So, be the change. Don't let yourself be controlled by money, people or your past. Find many reasons to keep you up, when a few things are there to bring you down. Remember, the direction is more important than the speed in life. Spend life with people who make you laugh and feel loved. Life is yours.

Live it to the fullest.

Real is more attractive than perfect. Creativity has more importance than perfection. Genuine is more valuable than perfect. Realise that imperfection is the perfect status of a human being. Modify your imperfections into creativity to find a different path to a bright future. When life is dragging you with difficulties, understand that it is going to launch you into something great. An arrow can only be shot by pulling it backwards.

Focus and hit the target happily.

This world is like a school. Each one of you is tested separately in different ways. That's the wisdom of the CREATOR. What's for you will always be there for you. So, relax and keep going through the beautiful tests and trials of your blessed life. When you desire new outcomes in life, you must break up with the old patterns. Better days are on the way. Live the new patterns of your dreams.

The world around you is experienced beautifully when you are at peace with the world within you. Relate to the universe to grab more signs to fix your journey in the right path. Do things for people not because of who they are or what they can do in return, but because of who you are. One day you will realise that material things are nothing. All that matters is your happiness and the acceptance of the people around you.

If you have ever been torn down to nothing but hope, you know exactly how powerful the word HOPE is. Rise up well. Heal abundantly. Exercise regularly and stay prepared. Your opportunities can arrive anytime. Always be ready to say goodbye to anything. No storm lasts forever. Be brave. Have faith. You are a winner.

You can never be good for everyone you meet in your life. But you can always be the best for someone who really appreciates you. Even if a single person is guided into peace and prosperity through you, realise that your life is a blessed one. Classy means even when you have a lot to say, you choose to remain silent in front of many. Start making room for what you have prayed for, because it's on the way.

Whatever happens in life, don't react arrogantly.

Anyone in this world can be arrogant. Real strength is your patience. Peacefulness is your guide. Forgiveness is your kind reality. If you allow these qualities in you, the help is always direct from the ALMIGHTY. Don't look at those who have more than you in these worldly affairs. Look at those who have less than you and be grateful. Realise the heaven around you.

Other people's negativity is not worth worrying about. Focus on your positivity. Aim at your attitude, dreams and goals. Allow yourself to have some joy. Forgive yourself and start loving the new real you. If you don't love yourself well, what else could be the most beautiful miracle of your life?

Sometimes, not getting what you want also can be a blessing. Everything happens for your goodness. The CREATOR knows what's best for you. Being kind to yourself is the best medicine. Life is a learning experience. Learn it happily and live it joyfully.

Life has challenges. Nobody said that life will be easy. Even the CREATOR acknowledged that life has trials and signs. To get on the pathway of understanding, the signs of the universe can be difficult at first. As you start practising and finding the signs with patience, it becomes easy. Except many humans, every creature of this planet and beyond follow signs. Sign" give the best answers even without questions.

Whatever happened in your life cannot be changed, undone or forgotten. Never regret anything more than needed. Never get stuck to your past. Consider everything as a lesson and move on to utilizing the current opportunities to achieve better results. Work hard but get leisure time at proper intervals. Be silent, but remember that wise people are not always silent, and they know when to be.

Be wise.

The most amazing place to be in this world is in someone's heart, in someone's thoughts, in someone's dreams, in someone's poetry, in someone's letters, in someone's memories, in someone's gratitude and in someone's journey to learn life. Have a beautiful and lovely journey of life.

Don't get stuck in any situation forever. Don't be sad forever. If you wish to make someone happy, consider yourself first. When you are joyful, you can create smiles in many hearts. Never feel like your heart will not heal. That is the greatest mistake. Seasons change. Everything in the universe changes. Then, why can't you be the change? Don't confuse seasons for a lifetime. Your worries have an expiry date. Grow, change, survive, smile and be the happiest one. Things will work out fine and well.

How to find a lovely you?
Help whom you can,
Love who you can.
Give what you can.
Forgive others.
Learn in silence.
Listen to the one who has nothing.
Care for the saddened.
Think before you speak.
Expect nothing.
Don't worry.
Live simple.
Embrace love.
You are beautiful now.

You cannot judge what someone is dealing with. The mind is like a magnet. When you focus on good things, you cultivate and nourish goodness. No matter how happy someone looks, how loud their laugh is, how beautiful their smile is, how kind their behaviour is, there can still be a level of hurt which is inexplicable. Choose to be kind to people. Choose to be silent without judgements. Silence isn't empty.

It's full of answers.

To gain something, you must lose something. That's the law of the universe.

A person who is hesitant to lose something will always get stuck in the past. One reason people resist change is that they focus on what they have to give up, instead of what they are about to gain. Have the courage to wave a goodbye. Then you will receive a new hello.

Never allow anyone to judge your path. Everyone has their own story and pain. Only you know how much courage and strength it took to rise up and continue to walk on until this moment. If you act right, it is for your own good, but if you are clinging on to mistakes, no one can help you except GOD. The best among people are those with patience. Always find a reason to laugh. It may not add years to your life but will surely add life to years.

The appearance of life to you is all based on how you view it. Think the best of it and it will unfold accordingly. Life is so much more beautiful when you stop explaining yourself to others. Just do what works well for you. Depression, anxiety and stress happen when you live to please others. There is no shame in making mistakes when you are learning life. The aim is to live a fulfilling life, not a perfect one.

The biggest mistake you make is that you are investing your dreams and love in others. Then you have to explain a lot about your viewpoints, and you reach nowhere. Invest in yourself. Realise that an insult to you is a great investment. That's a beautiful turning point so that you can turn the right way for you. Take the best turns.

People need your kindness a lot more than your opinion. Kindness is not a temporary increase in practicing righteous life, it is a glimpse of what you are capable of doing every day. Don't seek attention. Don't be concerned with being liked. Be comfortable in your own skin. Do what you say and say what you mean.

Don't be overly modest. Be consistent and practice what you preach. These are some important qualities of the awakened souls.

Never be worried or afraid to struggle. There is no shame in working hard to get where you want to be. Start your days happily and gratefully. Have small daily goals and attain them happily, peacefully and wisely. You may make mistakes. Forget it or leave it aside and try a different way to reach your goals. One day you are going to be celebrating something major. Be ready and be grateful right now.

Do not show interest in fighting, hating, blaming or being petty and arrogant with whatever time you have left on this beautiful planet. Not all storms come to disrupt your life, some come to clear your path. Don't chase people anymore. If they like to be with you, they will do so. Just be content in your own company. Work, live, love, help and be at peace. You are so special.

Every successful person has many painful stories. Every painful story has a beautiful ending when you don't give up. Accept the pain and get ready for success. The LORD has created each one of us with special abilities in the most special ways. Each of you have eyes, ears, a nose, lips, a face, hands, legs etc., but you never look the same. Even identical twins have some sort of difference. When your creator is so brilliant, why can't you use your brilliance to try your different abilities to create a beautiful life for you and the people around you.

Try a different approach and the results will be awesome.

Others don't have any right to judge your choices when they don't understand your reasons. So, explain everything in silence to the one who understands you, the one who created you, the one who gifted you a part of his own soul to make you alive and happy. He is your own ALMIGHTY. He listens to you and helps you by sending signs to guide you towards the right path in miraculous and lovely ways. Practice following his signs and you will find the real heavenly life on this earth.

When something seems to be going wrong, take a minute to remind yourself about all the other things which are going right. Don't get caught up on what could have been. If it should have been, it would have happened. Don't walk away from people to teach them a lesson. Walk away because you have finally learned yours. Enjoy every little moment in life because once they are gone, they won't come back the same. Live them well.

Align yourself with people that you can learn from, people who want to get more out of life, people who listen, people who have patience and people who love to live wisely and joyfully. Life is short and beautiful. Say what you wanted to say. Write what you have kept hidden in your heart and what you have learned from your life. If it helps someone else, you are so blessed. Select a good method to express yourself.

Work for a cause, not for applause. Live life to learn and express, not to impress. Be courageous to try a path which you find beautiful. The word TRY will be understood well, when you live it again and again. Courage doesn't mean you don't get afraid. Courage means you don't let fear stop you. Be positive.

When you are tired, give yourself a break. Don't make yourself depressed for the things you can't do. Don't feel guilty about not doing as much you normally would.

Don't chase love. Chase your goals and dreams. Those who love you don't go away. They walk beside you every moment of the day and night unseen, unheard but always near, deep in the heart, still loved, still missed and very near and dear. The ones who love you will never leave you.

One reason people hold on to memories so tight, is that memories are the things that don't change when everything else does. If the real change happens in people who are stuck with memories, life will teach them to accept and enjoy the moments wisely, and not to take any day, anything or anyone for granted. Get busy in trying new things to create the most beautiful out of now. Get the best out of your life. Keep trying.

Keep smiling.

Don't allow other people to hold the key to your peace of mind. Try to have the deepest affection for intellectual conversations. Strive for the ability to just sit and talk about love, life, anything and everything, but only to the right people. Trust your ability to become silent at the right time. Try to be alone rather than in a company of fake friends. Always be content in your own company. Then you are the strongest.

From the moment you start to distance yourself from people who hurt you, you will realise that life is getting more beautiful. Start living happily. For dreams, colours will be added again, without you even knowing it. Milestones of hope for your future will reach you. Greetings to the heirs of the good hearts. It's your time to shine. Get ready.

People were created to be loved and things were created to be used. The reason the world is in chaos is because, things are being loved and people are being used. When you love people, a bright light will shine from your heart. Carry that light within you throughout every day. Share your smile with others. Never ignore a person who loves, cares and misses you. One day you might wake up and realise that you lost the moon while counting the stars.

One day someone will walk into your life to prove why it never worked out with anyone else. Actions prove who someone is, words just prove who they pretend to be. Good or bad, everyone is sent to you as a special guest to teach you appropriate lessons. Live the days happily. Never go to bed mad. Be grateful to the CREATOR while you close your eyes every night, happily.

You must learn to say NO without feeling guilty.

Setting your own boundaries is a healthy behaviour. You need to respect and take care of yourself. As you become old, you become more honest and will not have time for pointless dramas. Be with the people who speak to you the truth. Trust your own inner guidance.

It knows the best.

The best kind of people are the ones that come into your life and make you see the sun where you once saw clouds. You start believing in yourself more, when you are with the people who believe in you. Those people will love you, simply for being you. The best lesson is not to force someone to make time for you. If they really want to, they will.

Realise how far you have come, not just how far you have to go. You are not where you want to be, but neither are you where you used to be. You will be there when you have to be. Trust that miracle and get ready. It's never too late to start over. If you weren't happy yesterday, try something new today. Don't get stuck. Do better every day. You have a long way to go.

Your happiness depends upon you. Don't expect someone else to give it to you. Fall in love with healing yourself. For your peace of mind, do not try to understand everything. Your life is a powerful one. When you fill it with positive thoughts, life will start to change. If you don't like where you are, move. You are not chained. Enjoy your freedom.

Life is about evolving too. Don't stay in any situation that is not helping you grow mentally, spiritually and emotionally. You've got to be mature enough to understand that you have some toxic traits too. It's not always other person's problem. Accept that while you move forward. Be grateful for every moment that you get to spend with the people you love. Life is a precious one.

Love all, trust few. Everything is real but not everyone is true. Live now and make it beautiful. Solo time is good for the soul. Appreciate growing alone. Survive alone to become the strongest. Not everyone you love will stay. Not everyone you trust will be loyal. Some people will enter your life as an example of what to avoid. Learn that aspect of life too.

Try to see things as they are today, instead of how you hoped, wished or expected them to be. If you don't allow yourself to move past what happened, what was said and what was felt; you will look at life through the old viewpoint. EVOLVE. Remember that everything happens for a reason. It might not make sense now, but at the right time, it will. Be at peace at the end of every day.

Time is not refundable. Use it wisely. Face everything and rise. Forget the hurt and move forward. Whenever you feel low or negative, remember how far you have come. Everything that you have faced, all the battles you have won and all the fears you have overcome were to produce the new you that you are now. Stay grounded with your roots. Enjoy your unique natural beauty. Keep glowing.

It takes a long time to reach the point of being completely unaffected by someone else's opinion about you. Your hard work and soul work cannot be taken away from you. It belongs to you. You belong to you. No one has the power to turn you ugly. Your every day is a gift. Open it, celebrate it and enjoy it. You carried yourself so well until this moment. Realise that it's not what happens to you, it's how you handle it.

Your destiny is not written for you, but by you!

Working hard for something you love is called passion. Go where you are loved and stay where it is consistent. You don't always need a perfect reason for doing everything in your life. Do it because you want to, because it's fun, because it makes you happy. Have a heart that loves to see people happy and succeeding. Life is a journey. Not a competition. What matter is your quality.

The older you get, you will realise that life is about finding peace, joy and contentment with people you love. Every moment has love in it. Every hour has happiness in it. If you lose it, it becomes memory. If you live it, it becomes life. Stop stressing. Take a deep breath. Everything is fine. You may not be perfect, but you are original. Keep finding the new signs every day towards your destination.

Every human has a past. Every saint today was a sinner in their past. Everyone makes bad choices in life and it's fine. None of the humans are completely innocent. But you get a fresh start every day to be a better person than you were yesterday. You cannot be perfect, but you can be loving and real. Be that beautiful you. It's quite possible things will turn out far better than you could even imagine.

Trust that process.

Dreams don't have an expiry date. People may judge that you lost.

Never mind. The person in your mirror knows you the best. He knows your capabilities given by GOD. If the mirror image keeps silent more than speaking, trust that the way is open. Dream more. Prepare well and wisely. A real winner is silent and steady.

He rises differently.

The letters become words, words become sentences, sentences become paragraphs, paragraphs become stories, stories become wisdom, wisdom becomes reality, reality becomes signs, signs become pathways, pathways become faith, faith become happiness, happiness becomes wings, wings help you fly, and you become humble.

When you are comfortable, growth is in a plateau phase. Attain maximum wisdom, patience and silence in that phase. Then look again for signs to move forward. Before you grab the chance of growth, trust the wisdom of ALMIGHTY. The most beautiful prayer is to become the one whom the ALMIGHTY loves. Be that one and you are safe.

Devotion is something which has to be understood apart from any explanations and arguments. A devotee in the right path is never alone. GOD always takes his side silently. The right and wrong can be judged in many ways. Remember, RUMI said: "Apart from the right and wrong there is a field, and I will meet you there." Believe in that beautiful field too.

Be the reason for someone's smile. Be the wind so that someone can fly. Be a butterfly of your own life. Be like an eagle when it rains.

Be like the earth in modesty. Be a student to achieve knowledge. Be a river to go with the flow. Be a rock to protect yourself. Be a leader to create a way. BE has great importance in this universe since GOD said, "BE YOU."

Don't be satisfied with stories. Humans are unable to know exactly how the world began. Live in the present by saluting the past to unfold your own myth of the future. The future depends on your ability to utilize the present chances in life. Find something new.

Live something new. Create something new. Be someone new.

Some victories are foreseen.

If you are chasing success, never let GOD out of equation. Add hope, confidence, patience, optimism and willpower at the appropriate turning points of the circle of life.

Life is a journey of circles or twisted circles. You will reach back to the same point where you started from the CREATOR. When he asks you how life was, say that:

"I lived it happily."

When you follow signs, understand that some of them are trials which might be mistaken for signs. In those circumstances, patience adds fruits to the journey to the eternity. Mistakes happen. It's a part of the journey. Don't analyse every sign. It costs a lot. Move on through those beautiful trials. You would find a way to the light of guidance.

If obstacles are large, jump higher. If it fails, relax and find another way to reach for a point far ahead of the place where you would have landed by jumping higher. That's a different kind of wisdom. Never try anything more than thrice in the same way. Miracles happen when you try something different. When you decide not to give up, ALMIGHTY will give you more.

When you realise that everyone's way is different, you never compare. Comparison destroys your actual self, and you get lost in sadness. It's your life and you are an important deciding factor in your happiness. When GOD gave you freedom, why do you have to live as a slave of humans and circumstances?

Wisdom arrives with experiences. Think, then ink your own thoughts and life.

Be in love with letters.

They become love letters.

You can live life in many ways. The best of all is the happiest and beautiful version. The choice is yours. It's your right to redefine your own happiness. Let me write to you a secret. Be the happiest version silently and never let anyone know about it, until you prepare your victory in a different way. Be a phoenix of your own making.

You won't separate and disrespect when you look at everyone around you as GOD's creation. Cultivate good thoughts for every circumstance. Appreciate the help. Smile at the goodness. Listen before you speak. Find your own way. Enjoy your own thoughts. Learn before you prepare. Prepare before you appear and realise without explanations.

Then, life is in heaven.

Thoughts are the results of experiences which you earn in life. Cultivate your thoughts into realities and nourish it with practice.

Follow what your heart says and find what your signs suggest. Hold on to faith. Relax and pause for a while. A small wise step in the right direction will create miracles. Walk until victory.

The rest will be history.

Make sure that you are in the company of people who touch your heart and nourish your soul. Don't be too quick to react to things. Weigh the consequences before putting thoughts into actions. Give yourself permission to change, heal, relax, rest and love. Silently, create a life that feels good inside you. There is no rejection in silence.

Be so confident in GOD's plan that you won't get upset when things don't happen as you planned. GOD works for the good of those who love him, who have been sent according to his purpose. If you are wise enough to understand that, schedule your priorities and seek an outcome that is beneficial to everyone. If so, satisfaction will be miraculous.

Happiness may be foreign to someone, but that doesn't make it less real. If you have the courage to fight for your dreams, realise that the doors are open. Pull yourself together and break the cage of your comfort. Create a path towards your dreams. You will live miracles if you embrace the unknown.

You can forgive people without letting them back into your life. The apology is accepted silently, and the access is denied happily. Not everyone you meet is meant to stay in your life. Some are blessings while others are lessons. Be honest in trouble, humble in wealth, silent in anger and polite in authority. If so, the help comes from the LORD.

Give people time and space to do what they need to do. You can advise and suggest, but you can't force anyone.

The universe has a way to process the present to proceed for the future.

Everything happens according to the great book of the LORD. The creation has to be in peace, so that they can understand and witness the great creativities of the greatest artist.

Try to be an open-hearted and kind person. It helps you a lot to move happily in life. Never separate based on caste, colour, creed, religion, position, profession, gender or money. When you separate, you are actually building a cage for yourself. That barrier is actually fixing limits on you by blocking your path towards the light.

Don't destroy yourself.

Sometimes you have to go through the worst to get the best. If you don't give up even when the calamity strikes you, life transforms into a beautiful pathway. You may have to walk it alone over a period, but that's fine. That walk might help you feel better, stronger, wiser and peaceful so that you will never give up life and dreams.

Be a great fighter.

Fix your visions forward on what you can do. Fix your heart on how kind you can be. Fix your brain on how you can think. Fix your ears on how you can listen. Fix your hands on how you can give. Fix your heart on how you can forgive. Fix your soul in peace and wisdom.

Finally, fix yourself just as a traveller to this world from the eternity. If you fix all these, some strangers can change the way you view and live life.

Fix your path uniquely.

Always remember that your current situation is not your final destination. Things will change and evolve when you change. Your greatest investment is you and your behaviour to the circumstances or people; a fact that helps you attain positions in life. Be the person you want to be, not the one others want to see. Then you may find a new you. Try it.

Be an energy to those who think they have lost. Be the courage to those who are determined not to give up. Be a fighter and fly out of the ashes. One day when you take your last breath, smile and leave the physical body to return only to the great soul. Until then you have time to win and to help others win.

Wishing you all the best.

Make your surroundings peaceful by getting away from negative people. Your happiness depends on how you react to your trials. Reach your daily goals wisely. A wise one never rushes to goals, as he knows that his goals will reach him. That occurs when you follow signs. The wiser the thoughts, the better is life.

Words are powerful. They leave a lasting impact. So, let nothing but good come out of your mouth. The effects will resonate far and wide. Words should be miraculously portrayed so that they heal, inspire, empower and encourage anyone who receives them. Words are chosen. Let ithem bring smiles to many lives.

Before, my beloved was like the wind. He touched the depths of my heart. He shined like the sun to give me light. He appeared deep from the dark like the moon to give me warmth. He became the pulse to live inside my heart. He became my eyes to see, my hands to write and my feet to dance. He called me friend and I called him GOD.

    The rest was silence.

As he began to write again, he realised that the memories, findings, pathways, signs, realizations, miracles and lessons were like an ocean. Surviving and resisting the onslaught of the waves, he moved on, searching, and finally finding the beautiful destination that is the calm ocean, deep inside him. All words were the result of his experiences and silences dancing through his fingers on the keyboard of his laptop, reaching the right ones who never wish to give up life, who wish to be different, who are kind and creative. If my silence gave you some strength, if it gave you some energy and a smile, my goal is complete. I wish you all a beautiful success.

May your next tears be tears of joy.
May your next years be so lovely.
May you achieve your individual heights.
May GOD guide you into your own realities.
May you shine always.
May you achieve your dreams.
You are special and beautiful.
With love,
Dr HANEESH KHANI.